After the Midnight Ride

by Anita Rochelle

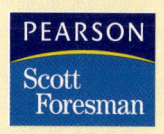

PEARSON
Scott Foresman

Editorial Offices: Glenview, Illinois • Parsippany, New Jersey • New York, New York
Sales Offices: Needham, Massachusetts • Duluth, Georgia • Glenview, Illinois
Coppell, Texas • Sacramento, California • Mesa, Arizona

Paul Revere rides on the night of
April 18, 1775, to spread the alarm.

*Listen, children from far and near:
You know of the night that Paul Revere
Galloped at midnight past village and farm
To warn every house and spread the alarm,
"The Regulars are coming out!"
That was Paul Revere's warning shout.*

Many people know about Paul Revere's famous ride. On the night of April 18, 1775, he rode from Boston to warn people that British soldiers, or Regulars, were coming. But there were really three riders that night: Paul Revere, William Dawes, and Samuel Prescott.

Paul Revere rode to Lexington. In Lexington, he warned John Hancock and Samuel Adams that the British were coming to arrest them. Then Revere, Dawes, and Prescott started riding to Concord. But on the way, they were stopped by British Regulars, who were also called Redcoats.

Samuel Adams (left) and John Hancock (right) were famous Patriot leaders. Like other Patriots, they believed that the American colonies should be independent and should not be ruled by the King of England.

A Redcoat (British soldier)   A Patriot (American soldier)

The British arrested Paul Revere.
Dawes got away but was thrown off his horse.
Only Samuel Prescott kept on the course
And arrived in Concord to give the warning
That the Redcoats would be there by the morning.

The Patriots were keeping many supplies in the town of Concord. They knew they would need weapons and food while fighting the British. But the British had learned about the supplies. They planned to march to Concord and destroy the supplies.

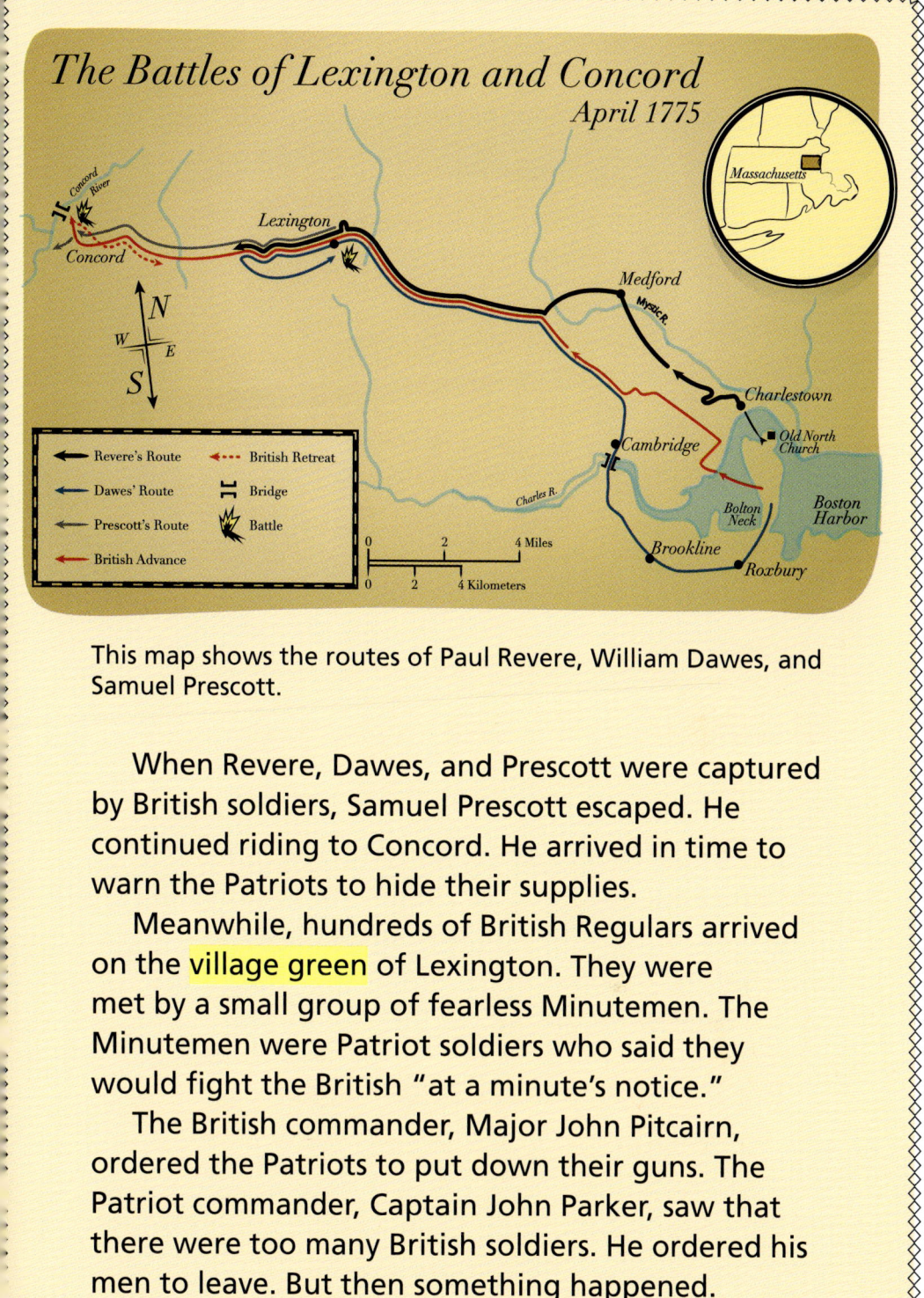

The Battles of Lexington and Concord
April 1775

This map shows the routes of Paul Revere, William Dawes, and Samuel Prescott.

When Revere, Dawes, and Prescott were captured by British soldiers, Samuel Prescott escaped. He continued riding to Concord. He arrived in time to warn the Patriots to hide their supplies.

Meanwhile, hundreds of British Regulars arrived on the village green of Lexington. They were met by a small group of fearless Minutemen. The Minutemen were Patriot soldiers who said they would fight the British "at a minute's notice."

The British commander, Major John Pitcairn, ordered the Patriots to put down their guns. The Patriot commander, Captain John Parker, saw that there were too many British soldiers. He ordered his men to leave. But then something happened.

---

village green: grassy park in the middle of a village or town

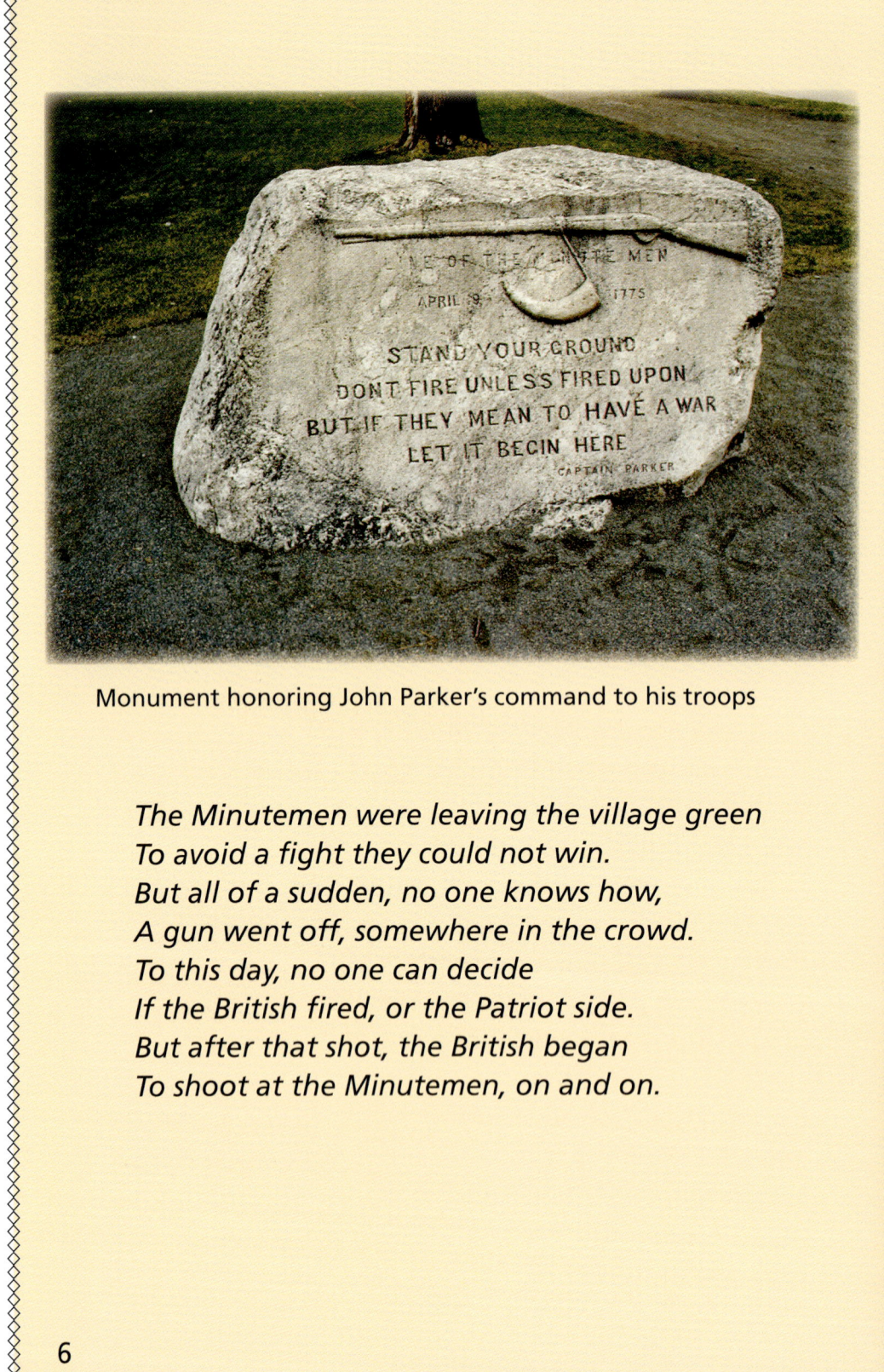

Monument honoring John Parker's command to his troops

> The Minutemen were leaving the village green
> To avoid a fight they could not win.
> But all of a sudden, no one knows how,
> A gun went off, somewhere in the crowd.
> To this day, no one can decide
> If the British fired, or the Patriot side.
> But after that shot, the British began
> To shoot at the Minutemen, on and on.

The Battle of Lexington was fought on the village green.

No one knows who fired the first shot at Lexington. But after that shot, the British began firing at the Minutemen. The Minutemen had been retreating, but they turned back to fight. Within a few minutes, eight Minutemen lay dead or dying.

The battle ended quickly, and the British Regulars continued their march to Concord. They thought their arrival would be a surprise.

But thanks to Samuel Prescott, the colonists were prepared for the British. They hid the supplies. Then hundreds of Minutemen from different towns gathered on a hill outside of Concord. They waited for the British to come for the supplies.

The British army leaves Lexington
To go to Concord for those supplies—
Muskets and cannon, tents, gunpowder,
Bullets, medicines, sacks of flour.
But the colonists there have worked all night
To get weapons and food out of sight.

An American Revolution cannon

---

muskets: old guns used at the time of the American Revolution

People today like to dress up and reenact, or perform, famous battles. These reenactors are dressed as Minutemen and are marching across North Bridge in Concord.

The colonists had done a good job of hiding their supplies. But some things were too big to move or hide. The British set fire to what they could find. The fire spread, and the Minutemen waiting outside of Concord saw the smoke. They thought the British were burning down the village. Hundreds of Minutemen marched toward the North Bridge of Concord, ready to fight.

British commander Walter Laurie was guarding the North Bridge with some Regulars. When he saw the Minutemen marching toward the bridge, he realized his troops were outnumbered. What would he do?

Minutemen rush toward British Regulars on the North Bridge of Concord.

The British see that they are outnumbered—
They can't possibly win. And for a moment
Nothing happens—the two sides stare.
A bird's song lingers and fills the air.
When, all of a sudden, a shot rings out
From the British side, without a doubt.
And then, once again, the British shoot,
Killing two Minutemen on the spot.

The British retreat from Concord as Minutemen shoot at them.

When the Patriot commander, Major John Buttrick, saw the British fire, he ordered the Minutemen to attack. The furious Minutemen chased the British Regulars back across the North Bridge. Three British soldiers were killed, and the British retreated to the streets of Concord.

The British soldiers decided to return to Boston. But by now the Minutemen had hidden themselves all along the road. As the Redcoats marched along, the Minutemen fired on them from behind trees, farm walls, windows, and roofs. Hundreds of British soldiers were killed or wounded. In one day, the first two battles of the American Revolution had been fought.

The famous painting *The Spirit of '76*

*More fighting takes place that April day,
In other places along the way,
But a dream is born, forever to stay:
A dream to be free to decide your fate—
The dream that made the Patriots great
When they answered the call that came so clear
With the midnight ride of Paul Revere.*